CW00385517

...from...
...ld ri...lly
...reams of......it
...ontaining an entirely
...ater. One is clear
...as rushed down from
...nother is clear but
...that its birthplace
...gst the peat; whilst
...nd deep, with muddy
...ly banks. It is
...and reeds and othe...
...has carned for itself
...name of Jon Beck.
...and

IMAGES
OF DALES LIFE
IN THE 1930s

Excerpts from the diaries of
Joseph Norman Frankland (1904-1995)

Frankland in Clapham, North Yorkshire

North Craven Heritage Trust

Images of Dales Life in the 1930s published by North Craven Heritage Trust, c/o Settle Town Hall, Cheapside, Settle BD24 9EJ.

© North Craven Heritage Trust and Elizabeth Shorrock

ISBN 0–9510071–3–0

All rights reserved. No part of this publication may be reproduced or transmitted in any form, or stored in any retrieval system of any nature without the prior written permission of the publisher, except for fair dealing under the Copyright, Design and Patents Act 1988. Full acknowledgment of publisher and source must be given.

Front cover: Haymaking at the farm of Mark and Alice Frankland, 1930s

Designed and printed by Pica Design & Print,
Burton Road, Low Bentham, near Lancaster, LA2 7ED.

CONTENTS

INTRODUCTION

In the early nineteen hundreds Joseph Norman Frankland was a boy living with his family at Middlesber, Austwick, a farm on top of a small hill between Austwick and Lawkland Mosses. He developed a keen interest in natural history especially botany. With growing knowledge gained from observation, books which he acquired and writing to various experts he soon became a skilful field naturalist.

On leaving school he went to Ingleton as an apprentice wood worker and this was to be his career for the rest of his working life. When he was working for a living, he moved with his family to Chapel House, Horton in Craven.

Spare time from work in winter was spent reading botany books, corresponding with people of similar interests, and mounting his growing collection of pressed wild flowers. At that time this was considered normal practice, to collect one specimen of each different flower. Now however, with the increasing decline of our native flora, it is no longer practised and in some cases it is illegal to pick wild flowers.

In summer he walked or hiked long distances, trying to discover some exciting new find, or confirming an old record. He would also check sites already discovered. Sometimes on his own, with a friend, or a group he would explore the countryside. Rubbish tips, old canals, deserted churchyards or any waste ground were investigated and often produced unusual and rare flowers.

One day in summer he decided to explore the Ainsdale Dunes at Southport. I now quote from an account by Fred Holder of his first encounter with J. Norman Frankland:

" 'Reg, there is a fellow coming along with a bag on his back!'

This remark was uttered by the writer on viewing a hatless youth plodding across a duneslack at Freshfield in the summer of 1926. We were, at that period, holding the status of Hon. watchers for the Royal Society for the Protection of Birds, which implies that we were thanked for our "invaluable services" and then promptly forgotten by headquarters.

The intruder was accosted and put through the third degree, while two pairs of eyes focussed on the haversack, it had a potential bulge which seemed to shriek "eggs". Much to our surprise the latter were not forthcoming, the stranger disgorged several botany books and some hard tack. We soon realised that in this wandering tyke we found a man after our own hearts. We made him welcome and softened his hard tack with a drink in our tent.

Together we have since basked in the genial sunlight of the dunes of S. Lancs and the Wirral. We have been soaked to the skin on the Sands of Dee. Ribblehead and Austwick Moss have given to us joyous hours, but to me my recent stay in the Craven Area must rank as pre-eminent for its sustained period of unalloyed pleasure among the real things of life."

This chance meeting was the start of a friendship that was to last for the rest of their lives. They spent holidays together, visiting each other's homes and they kept in touch with a regular correspondence. Both made notes of visits to various sites all connected with natural history. They gave each other nicknames:

Fred Holder – The Scribe

J. Norman Frankland – The Poet

Then they made a pact to write essays and to have them bound and made into books. Half came to be written by Fred, mainly about the Southport area, the other half by Norman about the Yorkshire Dales. The books are mostly about natural history but also teem with personal events in their lives – for example, both getting married – and with photos, poems, sketches and paintings. Norman also describes customs, memories of his boyhood and people he met during his life in the Dales.

The first book was for the year 1933, two each for 1934, 1935, 1936, 1937 and three hard-backed books told about two holidays they spent together. There are also in diary form, though not bound, volumes written by Norman for the years 1938 to 1945.

In retirement he lived in Thornton in Craven. When his wife Madge died he came to live in Newby near Clapham with his sister-in-law. He was still very active in his eighties and loved roaming around Newby, Clapham and Austwick, the area he knew so well. He was also a keen gardener. He died in

1995 aged 91. In his lifetime he saw many changes and, in writing them down, has recorded them for posterity.

I first met Norman when he was living in Settle. I had started taking an interest in wild flowers and he helped me with kindness and patience. He gave me the diaries, hoping that they would be looked after, not destroyed. Botany Recorder for the Craven Naturalists at Skipton, Warden of Colt Park Reserve at Ribblehead, Committee member of Craven Museum, and at one time author of a weekly article for the Craven Herald, he also led many walks for a number of societies. His herbarium is at the Liverpool Museum.

The Publications Committee of the North Craven Heritage Trust has selected extracts from those very extensive diaries that are of especial interest to the Craven area, but the last chapter charts Frankland's botanical trip to Devon, Dorset and Somerset at the invitation of Sir Maurice and Lady Abbot-Anderson – a challenging journey by motor-bike in 1931.

Elizabeth Shorrock

SCHOOL DAYS AT AUSTWICK

The extract forming this chapter starts with Frankland's schooldays, although it was written much later. He attended Austwick School for about six months, before leaving at 13 to work on his father's farm. He wrote this evocative piece in 1935.

Jill Sykes

In the very first essay written for these volumes I began at Austwick and have returned to Austwick more than once in them since then, even though the spot has not been in every instance specially mentioned. Again I go to Austwick, and once again in memory, a pleasure which is ever with me.

Austwick is not my native village, regardless of the newspaper reports I see whenever I give a lecture in the village, that it is. I was 13 years old when I first went there, so although not a native of Austwick I like to think that I am. Then again: I have to have a native village and which is it really? I was born at Hellifield, lived a few months there, a few months at Kirkby Malham, seven years at Stainforth, five years at Ingleton, and eight years at Austwick, by which time I was 21 years old. So from all these I pick Austwick as my native spot. Dad was from within a few miles of it, so why not?

By now you will see that this short essay is more or less a personal one. Personal things do not interest the man in the street but as these volumes are not for the man in the street what does it matter?

But to get to that title, I only attended Austwick School six months when I left and returned to work on Dad's farm before I was 14 years old. Since then any knowledge I have acquired has been because I wanted to learn. At school it was different. What did I care how much I learnt? True, throughout my school days I was usually first in the class, but not because I tried to be; it was sheer good luck.

I remember my first day at Austwick School. It was the forerunner of many halcyon days till the time I left. At playtime I was selected at once to be Horace Pritchard's horse, and a string of reins were duly tied round my arms. Horace still lives at Austwick, still unmarried, but still the same Horace. A good pal, keen in many ways, dull in others, but still one of the best. Whenever

I see Horace at Austwick now his opening remark is often "Does ter remember", then follows some lengthy reminiscence, the thought of which gives us both pleasure and takes us both back to carefree days long passed away. A Yorkshireman is Horace in speech and actions, but not the proverbial actions which are all a myth, exploded at once when one comes in contact with a genuine "Tyke". I don't think Horace will ever marry. Why I can't say. He loves his dog and gun, and he loves to roam the hills, but somehow I don't think the love of a woman will ever come his way.

Painting lessons caused great amusement. Roy Booth, a big happy lad, plastered paint all over the page, and we called these valiant efforts peep-shows. Roy has since married a cousin of mine and is a farmer pure and simple. Jim Bradley was a master hand at painting, and he and I shared the same desk. He is the only scholar, among those present then, who has made a name for himself above the ordinary. Leaving Austwick he had a few years at Skipton Grammar School; was on the staff of the Craven Herald for some time; and is now a reporter (very clever I believe) on the Yorkshire Post.

Future days were not dreamt of when I swapped pasties with Jim at dinner-times, for half the scholars lived some distance away and had to take the mid-day meal in a basket. I have never seen Jim for years and I wonder if he ever thinks of his school-days at Austwick in fustian breeches and clogs.

In summer we had an hour and a half for dinner, and what jolly times we had. Paddling in the beck near where the Cold Stream enters; tickling trout which we sold to village housewives; if we felt strenuous a long run of hare and hounds to the top of Norber and back; or a hefty game on the village green which we called 'Kick Can and Hook It'. In autumn it was many a run to Austwick Woods for a pocketful of nuts. No-one could spot them sooner than we boys, and no-one knew better where the most and finest grew. Autumn sunshine flooded the white scars, and gleamed on copse wood thickets taking on a brownish tint, as we made our haul and galloped back over the fields to school. Stiles and gates we heeded not, but went what is known locally as 'hedge and dyke'. Those nuts we cracked surreptitiously under the desk, splitting them open with a pen knife so as not to make any noise.

Life was an adventure to me then. Everything was full of romance. A love of nature was only just awakening in me slowly but surely. Bird-nesting time was the chief delight in this direction, an interest which has since led to higher and deeper things. Why should we be so hard on the bird-nesting instinct of a boy? Often it is a stepping stone to other interests which may lead to his achieving some beneficial work for mankind in one of the great branches of the Natural Sciences.

Austwick School – some pupils are wearing clogs.
The teacher on the left is Margaret Booth's late husband's grandmother.
© *Margaret Booth*

Trailing home across the fields of an evening (six of us went one way) we had many a jolly half-hour riding, without leave, Neddy Hodkinson's pony. Neddy is Dad's cousin. It was usually pasturing quietly in the field and was easy to catch. When caught we took turns at riding it, with one running alongside, hold of its topping. The two girls who went our way also got astride and we had a free ride. More than once one of us was thrown off its back, but that only led to more amusement for the others. The result was that we were often late home, but easily found an excuse.

Austwick School is of course a Church School, and the parson came now and again to see us, although the time had gone by when he held any sway and could give the children a holiday whenever he chose. In those older days the parson would come in on a Saint's Day and say, 'Now children, what day is it?' The children knew well enough by experience and replied in chorus 'St. Andrew's Day'. 'Who was St Andrew?' asked the parson. 'Our Patron Saint, Sir', answered the children. 'That's right children, and now you may have a holiday', and so they went home for the rest of the day. But Church School at

Austwick then, like all Church Schools now, was only a name, for the West Riding County Council has most to say.

There was a custom prevalent at Austwick School in those days that I have often wondered about since, as to whether it is still kept up or has sunk into the things of the past. Sometime I shall ask an Austwick schoolboy about it. I should think it had come down the ages from time immemorial. This was the custom for each lad (and lasses too) to kick the school door as he came out after breaking up for the holidays. In those days we got five weeks in summer. Each lad wore a hefty pair of Yorkshire clogs with iron heels which came up the side and as we streamed out we each gave the door a kick that shivered it and made the echoes ring. Everyone kicked it in the same spot so that a square foot of the door never had any paint on, and it was almost chewed through in that spot. Bang, rattle, bang, went the clogs as we streamed merrily out. The Headmaster (Mr Dent) closed his eyes to it. He knew that boys will ever be boys and never mentioned it. I don't think any master could have stopped it, however stern he was, and if it has died out it is through some other cause. Mr Dent, a fine chap and a master we all liked and respected, has long ago left his hobby of bee-keeping and crossed the Styx.

Schooldays now are different even at Austwick. They go to school in shorts, smart jackets, soft collars, and round school caps, although they still wear the clogs. In my schooldays we wore fustian breeches, jackets handed down from older brothers, cousins etc., stiff celluloid Eton collars that were sponged every morning, and big slouch caps or cloth hats. It was hateful to have to go to school for even one day in cloth breeches; one felt and was looked upon as almost half a girl. If our jackets were fustian too so much the better; and we were proud of it.

And so times change, but not always for the better.

Barnoldswick,
March 1935.

Picture of a boy at Austwick School in a fustian jacket

ELDROTH: AN OLD COUNTRY DANCE

At the time of this essay the first village hall was in use. The description of the event is followed by a list of dances performed at that time. Millennium year saw the replacement of the second old village hall by the present fine stone-built one. In 2002 an Irish evening continued the tradition of dancing in sets, at one of the well attended dances in the current programme.

Maureen Ellis

Many many years have passed since I last attended a country dance in a certain wooden hall at the foot of the brown fields that slope up to the moors. No doubt by now the new fangled slow motioned shuffling dances have gained a hold even there, but all the same old customs are bad to kill and even now I feel sure that should one go to the Farmers' Ball in that self same wood hut, there would be intermingled with the newer dances such old flings as Polka, Swinging Six etc. Before this wood hut was built, dances used to be held in a nearby barn where a wooden floor was laid for the purpose, but that was a generation previous.

At least twelve years ago it must have been. A kindly moon looked down from a cold yet kindly sky, on fields that slumbered under a winter night. Stars gleamed and twinkled over the calm still fields by the footpath, as we wended our way to the ball. Brightly Orion shone in the southern sky just as it does now, to all appearances, not one bit altered. I can see the whole constellation even now in mind as it was reflected from the slow moving waters of a marshy pool by the foot-bridge. It was past eight o'clock, the usual time for country dances to begin, and as we neared the Hall we could hear strains of music floating across the fields, and see the gleaming lights from the row of windows. The first dance, the invariable waltz had started.

We entered, hung up our coats on a peg along the side. Took off our clogs and pushed them under the seat, and donning our shoes we were ready for the fray. Everyone did the same, for it was the only place there was to put them. Not many couples were up, for although these country dances begin at 8.00p.m. it is not till at least 9.30p.m. that all the good folk from the far away farms by the edge of the moor have tramped the three or four miles to the 'stir', as a dance is locally called. No fancy streamers adorn the walls which are just washed with white and brown on the bare boards, and flickering oil lamps hang from the cross beams throwing a dim yellow light on the healthy faces of the happy throng.

Signpost at Eldroth, complete with O.S. map reference of its site. Photo: Maureen Ellis

On a little platform in the corner the band sits. Just a group of local musicians who more or less give their services. A piano however has been brought in from the school near by for the occasion. A lady plays the piano. Two or three young gents play violins, and an old chap, now almost blind tunes up by ear on a concertina. When the others go to supper the old chap keeps things going with his selections of old-time melodies. The music is of a great variety. Very old tunes follow very new ones, to which are danced old-time dances; but the time is very good indeed, and no one would be afraid of stepping gaily to it.

"Please take your partners" for the Quadrilles, Valeta, Turnoff, Polka etc. come in turn, but not till about 10.00p.m. does everyone get thoroughly warmed up to it. Then everything goes with a swing. Hot ruddy faces tell of the strenuous nature of the dances, as the deal floor swings to the rhythm of several hundred dancers. Some roll about like elephants, and some dance in a style worthy of the most up-to-date ballrooms. Tom Twistleton the Craven poet in one of his poems aptly describes such a dance.

"Thaar, back an' forrad, in an' out,
His elbow it gahs tiltin';
An' to an' fro, an' round about,
the dancers they are liltin',
some dance wi' eease I' splendid style,
wi' tightly-fittin togs on,
whal others bump about an t'while,
little drainers wi' their clogs on,
saa numb'd that neet."

I wonder how many people remember any of these dances? Some of them have been saved from the scrap heap by the Folk Song and Dance Society, and many have been picked up from the older folks of Craven and have since been danced in front of thousands in many parts of England. At the period I write about, it was only in a few very remote spots that many of these dances still lingered. In other districts in Craven they were not known except in the memories of the aged folks. Maybe I was lucky to have seen them danced as they actually formed part of the country folks' existence, and not in a now formal display that seems to me to be 'just pretend' of the older days.

Here tonight was a wonderful selection of dances, the like of which it would be impossible to see now at any country dance in England, no matter how far afield one went into the wilds. Lancers, Quadrilles – a square dance somewhat like the Lancers – Circassian Circle, in which the couples keep changing all round the room and spin up in fours. Swinging Six, when each man has two ladies one on each side, facing other three, and spins up first with one and then the other. Huntsman's Chorus, Turnoff and Sir Roger de Coverly, three dances very much alike where each couple in turn dances the whole length of the room in front of the others. Varsoviana, a slow graceful dance to an old time tune quite different from any other. Barn Dance, Schottische and Valeta with steps almost alike. Then there was the Highland Fling, Polka, Waltz, Grand March, Lancers and Kendal Gill. The waltz was of the old-time type and not the gliding dipping dance of 1934. It was steady with rhythm and motions, and the finest and best dance that ever was.

Many more dances besides these were danced that evening, but memory alone serves me now, so at least half of them have slipped away.

In the ante-room supper was ready and couples streamed in to dine as it were, not on sandwiches as thin as butterflies' wings, but beef and ham in manly slices to be eaten with knives and forks. Over this part of the 'stir' well fed farmers' wives presided, whose dancing days were almost over, yet who still liked to be present to do their bit. Once or twice during the evening a few of them would go through a set of Quadrilles or like dance, no doubt thinking the while of older dances still, that none of the younger folks would ever know.

The hours pass by till 4.00a.m. with no falling off whatever in the whole proceedings, then someone comes round with the hat, a collection for the band to play another hour. There were no restrictions in those days and no applications to be made for long night dances. Even up till 5.00a.m. things are just as brisk, and not till after then do folks begin to trickle away. "Please take your partners for the waltz, the last dance", is given out, and all who are left take part in a last fling. Some ready for off in hats and coats and iron shod clogs have a last spin thus attired ere they take the homeward trail across the early morning fields.

Good-nights and good-mornings fall thick and fast as the merry groups radiate from the dance hall door to return home, not to bed but merely to change into working clothes and start the day's routine by milking the cows. Weary, but contented many a farmer's lad falls asleep while milking as I have often done, only to awaken with a start and proceed. But it's worth it, and so they are there as brisk as ever at the next dance.

Daylight was tinting the eastern sky as we arrived back in the cobbled farmyard. Where had we been in those long ago days? Why to Eldroth, and only once of a score of times, and some day I shall go again to the same wood hut where the brown fields slope up to the moors, and dance again with the country folk as I did long ago.

But I'm afraid I shall feel out of place. The dances will have changed, and the people. Maybe it will bring more sorrow than joy to me. Pleasant memories of faces now no longer there will bring with them a touch of sadness, and show me so vividly how the years have altered and acquaintances got squandered about.

Only last week I read of the Farmers Ball being held there, and somebody or other's 'syncopated band' arriving by motor from some place many miles away. So perhaps after all I had better not go to spoil the sweet memories of old-time dances with the country folk I used to know – then.

Barnoldswick, February 1934. Joseph Norman Frankland.

OLD TIME DANCES OF CRAVEN

Varsoviene or Varsoviana
Square Eight
Turnoff
Black Joke
The Cottagers
Swinging Six
Butter & Peas or Buttered Peas
Steal the Lady (Triumph of English Folk Song & Dance Society)
Quadrilles
Lancers
Highland Fling
Circassian Circle
Polka
Sir Roger de Coverly
Barn Dance
Valeta
Schottische
Brass Nuts
Waltz
De Albert

ROEBURNDALE: MY WARTIME MEMORY

This sad and emotionally written piece displays a very human Frankland, whereas his botanical writings are dispassionate and scientific. The surname of Jack remains unknown. The photograph is of the War Memorial tablet in Wray Church near Roeburndale and it would be pure conjecture as to whether it provides the answer.
Maureen Ellis

Those War years. How far away they really are now, and yet how near in the minds of those who were old enough to realise it all. Almost sixteen years have passed since the last gun boomed in Flanders, and many young men and women of today can understand nothing whatsoever about those fatal years. Most of us who are old enough to know, have at least one memory that cannot but oft be recalled whether we will it or not of someone who:

"Died not for King nor Flag nor Emperor
But for a dream born in a herdsman's shed"

Some maybe, died not even for a dream, but died for nothing at all.

When science (shame on it) was blowing human lives to pieces in Flanders. When British ships were battering British built fortifications in the Dardanelles. When one army was blazing away at the other with ammunition made by countrymen of the chaps they were shooting at, England looked just the same. That is the England away from the towns; the England of the fields, woodlands and moorlands. Nature heeded not the guns in Flanders fields, but came into life each spring as fresh and green and inspiring as ever. Thus it was, that when I awoke one bright spring morning in an old Manor house in Roeburndale, the world seemed so beautiful. It was a morning such as only a spring morning can be in England. Brilliant sunshine flooded the walls, and through the open window came the cheery chorus of the birds from the nearby garden, and coppice woodlands that grow so thick and luxuriant for miles and miles along the steep banks of the stream.

Who could stay in bed on such a morning; least of all a boy. For the birds were busy nesting everywhere, and that, in those days, and in May, was all I cared to think about. Out on the dewy grass beneath the orchard trees I wandered before breakfast, and along the side of the dreamy lake by the old manor house. Rhododendrons bloomed down the side of the old drive. Daffodils gleamed golden on the grass, and tulips of many hues filled the air with a sweet orange-like odour.

I had a companion. A slim youth of eighteen. In mind just a boy as I was, full of the glamour of springtime and birds-nesting and all the beauty around us. He wore a khaki uniform with brightly polished buttons, and although he was a soldier yet that did not deter him one wit from being a boy full of fun and energy that urged him on like the boy in the poem:

"Up the river and o'er the lea"

Maybe it was 1916, maybe later, I do not know. Nor do I care to know exactly. All I wish to remember now is Jack as I last saw him, roaming the fields and woods, climbing trees and wading streams in his suit of khaki. With things like this why should one be exact; the time has long passed, and

War Memorial, Wray Church. Photo: Maureen Ellis

19

accurate details do not enhance the memory.

A Yorkshire farmhouse breakfast we enjoyed together. Porridge and home-fed bacon, and the sun still streamed through the windows. Then - what a glorious day we had. Scrambling through the woods in search of woodcocks which abound there. Over fields and streams, then away to the moors. This Roeburndale is as romantic as its name, and teems with wildlife. That jolly day we had our full share of it, for to us the world was young; we were both, so to speak, but schoolboys. We saw too many things for me to remember them all. I remember the whole jolly day in one – and most of all – Jack, with his carefree boyish ways, little dreaming that he really formed part of a great selfish and tragic organization.

A few days later when I had returned home Jack left Roeburndale forever. A few weeks later in Flanders Fields he left everything forever. And now, to me, is, more than any other:

"One corner of a foreign strand
This is forever England"
(Misquoted from Rupert Brooke's poem, *The Soldier.*)

Barnoldswick,
May 23rd 1934.

MIDDLESBER: THE LOST COW

Norman Frankland knew this area between Lawkland Moss and Austwick Moss extremely well, as he spent several years at Middlesber Farm, the centre for the following article. The landscape has not changed a great deal in the intervening years; in fact nature has taken over some of this land creating further hazards for the unwary traveller.

Roy Gudgeon

It was a wet day in autumn, but exactly what month I cannot very well remember now. I know that it was well after the hay harvest had been gathered in, for the lush aftermath or 'fog' was thick and green in the meadows.

Had you said anything about it to a Craven farmer he would have told you that the meadows were 'groshy'. Often dialect words that have lingered on from the ancient lingo of our forebears are very apt, and no word in our present vocabulary so justly describes this meaning. Grosh, or groshy, means lush, luxuriant, full of moist green-ness and life, in anything that grows, and surely no other word can describe it so concisely and so accurately.

The damp warm drizzle that lay like a rich draping curtain all around, blotting out the hills made the meadows and fields look so green to the eye in the dull light. It was milking time at the farm on the hilltop and the lad had gone down to the level meadow beside the 'moss' to bring in the cows. Lassie, the brown dog, flew round them like an arrow without any more telling than the 'howp, howp', as the boy's call echoed back from the scarcely visible pine trees in the wood nearby. Only nine cows came out of the misty drizzle; there should have been ten. The boy walked round the meadow hedge but saw nothing of it, nor even a break in the hedge where it might have broken through, so drove the other nine up to the farmhouse on the hill top.

It was a very serious thing to lose a cow at this farm, for all around lay treacherous mosses full of deep peat bogs, ditches and morasses of sphagnum moss, and a cow or other animal once fast among them was often there for all time. In this part of this particular valley it was a common thing for one farmer to call others to his aid to help dig out a cow fast in the swamp.

Sometimes they were freed with the aid of ropes and spades, at other times three-legs and blocks had to be brought into use, whilst occasionally the only way to be done was to bring a gun and leave the wallowing carcass whatever its worth to rot away amid the rank vegetation. Even some of the meadows were so soft that pattens of wood were often fixed to the feet of horses whilst mowing unless the weather had been very dry.

Hence the anxiety at the farm, milking was hurriedly rushed through, and the search began. Neighbours were informed and some half dozen boys and men set off in the drizzling rain armed with ropes and spades. Even old Jimmy from Bark Head donned his heavy coat, and leggings, and ploughed his way among the tussocks and peaty pools of the surrounding marshlands. Each went in a different direction, for some square miles had to be searched, and each knew from past experience what a shrill whistle coming through the mist meant. Maybe the sight of the lost cow safe and sound - maybe hours of strenuous digging and pulling, or maybe a black churned bog and an animal beyond recall, whatever it was it would mean some sight of the cow.

Everyone knew the cow they were looking for, for most farmers know by sight any animal belonging to another man in the vicinity, so deep is the interest and so good the memory as regards live-stock. But this cow was better known than most and was always called "t'funny coloured 'un" for it was one of the queerest coloured, or rather queerest marked cow that ever lived. It was half roaned, half grizzled, and with barred stripes on each side after the style of a tiger or zebra. One horn pointed upwards, and the other downwards.

This was no time to discuss the merits of "t'funny coloured 'un", but a lone trudge for each seeker through bog and mire, so wet that even the stoutest north country clogs could not withstand it all day. In the bogs, vapour seemed to curl up from the dank pools and mingle with the floating curtain all round. Wild ducks rose from the ditches and flapped away to pools beyond. In the pinewoods the mist hung around the pools so thickly that the woods seemed almost dark, and rabbits driven from their haunts on the moss-land had found shelter, snug and warm in tufts of fern. Tall foxgloves peered through the gloom, like tall purple sentinels amongst the wide green fronds. Glancing sideways the farmer saw in one bog the white bleached ribs of a horse protruding from amongst the trailing Marsh cinquefoil. Well he remembered the hours of struggle in which he had taken part only to be given up as futile, and £60 had to be left to rot. It was not his horse however, but the cow was.

After hours of patient searching the seekers returned, tired with struggling amongst the bogs, and wet to the skin. Several big sheep-dogs shook their shaggy coats and stood around with hanging tongues, as well aware of all that was taking part, so it seemed, as their masters. The cow was lost and perhaps buried out of sight by this time.

But "t'funny coloured 'un" was not dead, it was very much alive, for it was found accidentally some days after patiently cropping the 'grosh' grass in a meadow over the marshy stream about half a mile away. To get there it had crossed a number of deep treacherous ditches, much treacherous marsh, and a deep slow running stream. How it got there will never be known, but the farmer thinks it must have crossed a narrow plank bridge over the stream and into the meadow. It left no trace whatsoever, but was duly garnered in, and the rain drenched tramping of the previous day was forgotten, and went down to posterity as one of the everyday occurrences in this marshy part of the valley.

Barnoldswick,
January 1934.

MIDDLESBER: PEAT AND POTATOES

Peat is the accumulation of humus such as sphagnum moss, sedge, ling, and tree stumps in the water-logged soil where evaporation failed to keep pace with supply of water.

The cutting and drying of peat developed and two words came to be used. The first is peat or pieces, and the second turf or turves. Commoners exercised and still do sometimes the right of cutting peat or turves from a turbary. The latter word is from turba, lawyers' latinization of turf. Peat was used for smelting lead, burning in lime kilns and by blacksmiths. Enormous quantities were used in smelt mills, but it is as domestic fuel that it is remembered and Norman Frankland wrote and took photographs in the 1920s of peat pits, and the drying process. He also described the tradition of potato growing on peat.

Maureen Ellis

On the Moor

Down in the hollows it is wet and swampy, with old peat bogs full of tall green rushes and water, black and stagnant with standing so long amongst the peat. Many farmers come yearly for peat to burn in their homes; but before it is taken away it has to be dried, and for this reason it is set up – two pieces leaning against each other – for the wind to blow through it.

Austwick Moss

Who does not love a ramble in the marshlands even though the ground is rough and boggy, and every minute one stands a good chance of getting wet. Here everything grows of its own free will, everything is truly wild and wild creatures are very numerous. This marshy tract is situated in the centre of the wide dale; in the district they are called mosses, probably because many species of moss grow in profusion on them and the soil is peaty.

For quite a long way we may walk through an almost never ending stretch of peat bogs from which peat has been dug by the inhabitants of the district in ages past, to burn when there was little or no coal available. Some of them measure only a foot or two across, while others stretch for fifteen or twenty yards. Most of them are full of dark brown water, in some places as deep as eight or nine feet, and to get along we must skirt carefully round them on narrow grassy ledges which shake beneath our feet.

Photo from Frankland's Diaries of potato beds in the peat

White feathery tufts of cotton grass nod in the wind. Bilberries hang over the water in bunches, and in many places black crowberry carpets the edges of the deep dark pools for many yards with its evergreen leaves. Besides the bilberry and crowberry we can find plenty of variety of wild fruits on the marshes. Where the ground rises a little and is fairly dry the cowberry grows. Redshank has always been one of my favourite birds, and the marshes would not seem half so lovely in Spring, if they were without such beautiful and harmless birds. In the winter the marshes are the haunts of many species of wild duck and wild fowl; the little jack snipe haunts the bogs, black grouse may be seen perched on bushes and fences, and red grouse come down from the fells in snowstorms. Wild geese often settle in the marshes, and huge flocks of wild duck are to be seen, chief amongst them being teal, mallard, goldeneye and widgeon. Although I have seen tufted ducks here in Spring, I have never yet been successful in finding a nest of that species.

In some parts of the marshes where the soil is wet and peaty the farmers set potatoes in a very curious style called the lazybed way. Although called the lazybed style there is nothing lazy about it as I can say from experience. They are set in beds which are six feet wide, and between each bed is a ditch two feet wide. Instead of being planted in a place ready dug for them they are simply laid on the grass one foot apart. Then the ditches are made up each side, the slabs of peat being placed over the potatoes on the grass, half of the ditch going one way and half the other. The top is then pushed a little with a fork as a means of keeping the moisture in and to give them a straighter appearance. They are then finished until ready for getting up as they need no hoeing at all as very little weed grows on them. The ditches fill with water and this soaks up through the peat and keeps the potatoes moist. Potatoes are only set on one patch of ground for two years, the second year after being levelled the ditches are made up to the centre of the old beds and the potatoes planted over the old ditches. After two years new ground is selected and the old patches left to grow as they will.

It is very interesting to notice the different vegetation that grows in different stages on the old potato beds, before it reverts back to the former tough

Photo from Frankland's Diaries of peat drying before being set up

marsh herbage. The first year after being left there is scarcely anything but docks growing almost a yard high. Then hemp nettle comes and charlock, knotweed, goosefoot, thistles, nettles , black bind weed and weeds innumerable each taking their turn of being master of the plot. Each year more rushes and rough grass get intermixed with the weeds, until eventually they get stamped out.

Whilst the ditches are being dug for the potatoes, many sorts of wood are got out of the peat. Some of it may have lain for hundreds perhaps thousands of years, and most of it is just as hard and sound as it was on the day it was buried. The chief kinds of wood found here are larch, scotch pine, willow, birch and oak. Willow and birch are generally rotten when found, and a curious thing about birch is that the wood is often rotted away while the bark remains sound and is left hollow like a drainpipe. Scotch pine has generally plenty of sound bark left on it but the wood is sound as well, while larch and oak have scarce any bark left on them. At the present time in a certain low-lying meadow a huge trunk of oak is being dug out and will have to be hoisted with blocks. It is a yard in diameter and perhaps twenty yards long, and ought to be worth a good lot when procured.

Here in one of the bogs is the white and weather-beaten skeleton of a horse with the ribs sticking up gaunt and bare. It is all that is left of a noble steed, and it reminds us that those marshes have a sorrowful and tragic tale to tell as well as a beautiful and happy one. Cattle, sheep and horses, especially the two former, often stray through the old fences on to the boggy places and get stuck fast in the soft ground. Most of them are seen and rescued, but now and then one dies, or kills itself trying to get out before it is found, and soon only the bleached bones are left to tell the tragic tale.

Middlesber.
Originally written in 1920 and
copied out by Frankland in 1940.

OLD NEDDY CLARK

Neddy Clark was a real character who spent most of his life in the area around Austwick, Clapham and Lawkland. Very little is known of his early years, but we know that in his later life he was 'requested' to leave his rented accommodation in Lawkland and, to show his disdain for the landlord, it is recorded that he dug up all the half-grown potatoes in the garden, rather than leave them in the ground for someone else. He then lived for a while in an old cottage that is no more in Eldroth, which was once the house and workplace of a local blacksmith. The photograph of Neddy Clark shows him in Austwick, close to the old pound which disappeared long ago in the march of progress!

Roy Gudgeon

Long ago, but not so long ago that I cannot remember it, when grasshoppers twittered, or rather chittered in the mossy fields the whole long summer day, an old chap used to come hobbling over the field-way to the village each week to draw his old-age pension. Winter and Summer alike he came with his knot stick and his faded old plaid. In summertime or when the weather was warm and fair he carried his plaid over his arm but in wet weather or in winter time it was thrown about his shoulders. His plaid had seen better days, for once long ago, it had held all the bright glorious colours, as bright as those on the plaid of an old-time Highland chieftain, but now, so many rains had beaten against it, that the colours were wan and faded. Still it was serviceable, and maybe it could turn the wild weather as well as ever.

Once upon a time nearly all the men folk in Craven wore plaids instead of overcoats, so it must not be thought that Neddy was in any way Scotch. No, he was a pure Yorkshiremen like many another that preceded him and the tartan plaid for generations has belonged just as much to Yorkshire as to Scotland. Thrown athwart an old countryman's shoulders there is something rather romantic about it, for it speaks of the wild heather-clad moors that sweep in graceful curves over such a wide expanse of Northern England. Perhaps somewhere on the skirts of the Craven Moors a few lingering plaids are still in use, but for the most part they are gone like a tale that is told and the generation that follows mine will not be able even to remember.

Neddy Clark, early 1900s

Why do I write of Neddy Clark? Not that he was anything outstanding really, or had any special characteristics because long ago there were hundreds of Neddy Clarks in those valleys of ours, but most of them have gone now, and Neddy, when I knew him was one of the last of the old time plaid brigade. His passing for the sake of his plaid alone has almost if not quite snapped another link between these modern times and the days of our forebears.

We feel sad about these things passing away, and whatever we say about the matter we shall still feel sad. In Yorkshire as well as elsewhere other things are passing. In the industrial areas we see the passing of the clogs and shawl, and though it perhaps is all for the better, there is still a sadness in it, perhaps more for the associations than the things themselves.

Maybe I write about Neddy because around him cling such a lot of pleasant memories, of a pleasant period, in a pleasant spot which will ever bring back happy thoughts to me. Not that he had any direct influence over them, but just that he was there and about at that time. To think of Neddy placidly stumping along the foot-path, through the brown tangled grass of the pastures by the Mosses calls to my mind many things that are good to think about. Often he would come along as Dad and I were at work in the fields. Everything he knew and everything he talked about was of the fields and moors. I doubt if he had ever been further afield than ten miles from his native hearth. Anything to do with towns was a complete blank to him.

Like most of these old stagers he knew everyone for miles around. He could tell you who married so & so and when. How long a certain farmer had farmed a certain farm and all the other things that are only interesting to local people. But it was his 'lingo' that interested me most. The dialect that he had been steeped in from childhood, and the dialect that he would use till he died – and maybe after. Many of the words he used no doubt would die with him and a few other old timers of his generation. I doubt if many south country people could have understood a word he said.

About his past life I know nothing except that it must have been spent mostly out of doors at one occupation or another, and that it was all spent in the nearby countryside. Perhaps at a guess he had picked up many pennies by the sale of game, poached when most people were sound asleep, for he was an adept at snaring and catching rabbits and other wild saleable things in a variety of ways. He had never been married, and lived by himself in an old tumble-down cottage at Eldroth. He kneaded and baked his own bread, washed for himself and bred ferrets by the score in the back kitchen. They were the only company he had at home.

How many memories must Neddy have had as he sat at home in the gloaming, or by the light of a flickering oil lamp. Left there by himself, the last of his generation. All the friends of his youth had gone, and the new ones are not like the old; they are too young to see life from an old man's angle. I often think of him when I think of the time when such a thing may happen to me if destiny allows me to live to a ripe old age. The memories must be grand to ponder on, but the sadness of them almost unbearable.

I wish I had taken a photo of Neddy in his billycock and plaid when I had the chance, but it is too late now. Since I left the old spot Neddy has gone, and now lies amid the remains of his own beloved generation. His old tumble-down cottage is now no more. The last time I passed that way it was not even a ruin, for nothing but the grass grown foundation remained. Soon he will be entirely forgotten, and the name of Neddy Clark will mean nothing at all to anybody in the district. To me it means a lot and always will do.

The grass grows over the ruins of Neddy Clark's cottage just as it grows over his grave, and up the roadside just above come botanists each year to a colony of marsh orchids that gladden the roadside in June with their purple flowers. The botanists know nothing of Neddy, just as Neddy knew nothing of the orchids save that they grew by the roadside above his tumble-down cottage long ago.

1944.

A DYING CRAFT – OLD JOE STOUT

The village wheelwright is passing away fast and soon will be merely an echo of village life. True, there are many village joiners who can do a bit of this sort of work; but there are very few of the old type left – the old slow-motioned, hardworking country wheelwright, proud of his work and his traditions.

Old Joe Stout was one of these, and one of the last of his type. Some ten years ago he passed away in his native village under Ingleborough. Wilson was his real name, but everyone knew him as Old Joe Stout. He was not at all stout, but this name had been derived from his fondness for the flowing bowl. In his later years this scarcely interfered with his work, but he knew of the time when all workmen were excused on Monday mornings to arrive at their own time. Every now and then most of them would 'strike the rant' to use a local expression. For days, sometimes more than a week, one or more would disappear, and if a search had been made they would have been found at some pub in a not-too-distant village 'drinking, drinking, drinking' till all the money was done. Many's the time Old Joe had 'struck the rant' in his younger days.

There is something sad about old times, old folks, old customs, and old crafts, which are forever passing away, but perhaps it is all for the best as we sincerely hope the world is improving, and perhaps reading about these things is far easier than living among them. Old Joe was about seventy when I first knew him, and it was then that I worked as an apprentice under him for a fair long time. He was well known in the district as one of the best, if not the best wheelwright within a big radius of the village, and farmers and others came for miles with carts, traps and wagons for Old Joe to repair and deal with in his superior way.

'Master of his craft' he was and everyone knew it was so, and his practical eye could see at a glance every defect in a wheeled vehicle. And his deft fingers could fashion a wheel on a wagon so true and strong that it would last a lifetime.

I can see him now coming down the village street to his work. His old putty-smeared billycock stuck slantwise over his head, and his long white apron folded up in a roll under his jacket. His hands thrust deep in his trouser pockets and a long curved pipe protruding from between heavy side whiskers. He was only a little man and his legs were slightly bowed, but everyone respected him, and as he puffed at his pipe and sauntered along, he would be met at frequent intervals by "mornin' Joe".

Sometimes, when we were to work out, he came on his bicycle. When on it he was all right but sometimes when dismounting he failed to lift his leg high enough. At such times, there was a flop and a crash, the bike flew one way and Old Joe flew the other, and although I have seen him fall off in this way many times, he always landed on his feet. In his early days he was a lish, agile man and although his legs were stiff with age now, he still kept a good deal of his agility. Once long ago he was at the top of a 30ft. ladder pulling a hold-fast out of the wall. It came out rather quicker than he expected, and the ladder and he flew backwards. But he landed on his feet as he always did, like

A wheelwright at work. From the collection of Marie Hartley at the Dales Museum, Hawes

a cat, very little the worse.

When Joe built a cart it was a cart. Put together slowly and accurately until it was turned out bright and ready for use in its coat of rich orange-coloured paint lined with black. Nothing but the best would Joe use. Every piece of wood he handled had to be thoroughly seasoned and perfect. It was looked at, talked about, and tested – crudely but nonetheless accurately – before he began work on it to form part of the finished cart or wagon.

Practically all timber used in oldtime cart construction was English grown. The framework was of oak, the shafts of ash, the sides and boards of larch. The axletree of elm or ash, the naves of elm or oak, the spokes oak, and the felloes or wheelrims ash. Joe preferred elm to oak for naves, as he said it did not respond to the weather so soon, and so avoided loose rattling spokes in summer.

The wood was felled locally and laid for years in the wheelwright's yard before it was cut up into planks which were again stacked for several more years until thoroughly dry. The cutting of the trees into planks was performed by hand in saw-pits, one man underneath in the pit, and one above, saw-saw-sawing day in and day out – work it was I can tell you, and Old Joe knew it. Many of these old saw-pits are still to be seen lying derelict in wheelwright yards never to be used again – long deep built-up pits, and here and there one sees the old tapering saws once used, corroding away on a hook by the wall. Occasionally when wandering in Craven one comes across an old-time village worthy who has oft sweated in his youth in the bottom of one of these pits. Soon even these lingering dalesmen will only be a memory, and nothing will be left but the tumbledown pits to speak for themselves as best they may.

It is grand to think about Old Joe, as he sat astride the stock in the wheelwright's shop, bumping away at a pair of naves as he morticed them well and truly, each hole true to one thirty-second of an inch – or less. Then with pride he would stand up to survey his handiwork. Nor was he backward in explaining all the little intricacies of the trade to me his pupil, but he was always firm in the opinion that all marks should be planed off or buried in mortice holes to keep the secrets of the craft inside the building.

The building of carts in the old way has almost gone. Each wheelwright had more or less his own pattern, and own peculiarities of adornment, and in each village down the generation this was strictly adhered to. Old Joe could tell at a glance where a cart had been made, or at least the district up to fifty miles away. This keeping to type did not change rapidly from village to village but across the countryside one form merged gradually into another. The further up the Dales one went the smaller were the carts, owing to the rough mountainous ground.

Old Joe Stout and many another old craftsman like him has gone never to return, and now many village wheelwrights, instead of building wheels in the good old-fashioned way, merely send away to some wholesale firm and buy the wheels – machine made – ready for fixing. Many carts now have the boards and sides of pitchpine or larch from Archangel – even some of cheap redwood from Northern Europe. The spokes too are often made of softer oak from Russia. I wonder what Old Joe and others like him would think of this.

Motor vehicles have almost pushed the horses off the road. Carts are now used practically only for field work and so do not need to be built to stand the centuries. Furthermore, most farmers could not afford to pay for such solid building, or even yet the oldtime wheelwrights would still exist. Many wheelwrights now own a garage attached to the old shop, and have turned their attention to motor body building and repairing.

Yes, times have changed, and let us say that all we hope is that they are for the better.

Barnoldswick,
October 1933.

HAYMAKING
At the farm of Alice and Mark Frankland
Long Gill Farm, Wigglesworth

HINKLEHAUGH

Both essays which follow describe expeditions, about 20 years apart, to Rye Loaf Hill, a distinctive summit near the Settle – Kirkby Malham road. The first was a social occasion in the company of Mark Frankland, a cousin of Norman and known to him as Marcus, who farmed at Long Gill, between Rathmell and Wigglesworth. The second is an account written for the Craven Herald, of an outing with the Craven Naturalists.

Harold Foxcroft

J ust a bit of sun, just a bit of wind from the West and a free day before us. Thus we started on foot from Settle – Marcus and I – to tread some Craven ground untrodden by us, and to set foot on one of Craven's most conspicuous peaks, from which one of the finest views is to be had. This was Rye-loaf, high up between Settle and Malham. It is so called because it looks like a gigantic old fashioned loaf of rye bread. On the older maps and in old books it is known by a much more romantic name, Hinklehaugh, and why it should have been changed to Rye-loaf is past the comprehension of any romantic mind. Therefore, henceforward I shall call it Hinklehaugh. The word Hinklehaugh is well fitted to stand besides such full-sounded names as Ingleborough, Pen-y-ghent, or Whernside which Rye-loaf is not.

The wild white hills above Settle were flecked with scurrying patches of sunshine, and the wind rustled through the brown grass tufts and rough built walls that climbed about at all angles on the steep slopes. The old Roman encampment stood just as it stood in years gone by, seemingly as everlasting as the hills that surrounded it, and the big dew-pond below lay unruffled by the wind that fanned the hill tops and missed the hollows.

By Scaleber Force the sun felt warm as we passed the sheltering trees, but on the moorland above the wind rushed by, sweeping the bare tree-less hillside clean and sweet. In the tiny runnels watercress flourished though few other flowers were out up here so early in the year. Curlew and cuckoo filled the air with song, and as we rose higher so the wind gained in power. Yellow mountain

*Mark
Frankland by
the cairn on
Hinkelhaugh
May 13, 1934*

pansies dotted the ground about us, and by some tiny pot-holes the rich green of ferns brightened the grey rocky sides.

A last steep climb brought us to the top of Hinklehaugh, 1794ft. above sea level, and behind the cairn we sheltered from the wind which blew a hurricane. A view that was wondrous fair lay before us. The Craven mountains reared themselves up to the north; the Bowland Hills to the west; southward we gazed across the Craven Lowlands to Pendle Hill, and further towards the east we descried the white road over Greenhow Hill to Pately (*sic*) Bridge. Nearer, Kirkby Fell, a few feet higher than Hinklehaugh, hid the fair vale of Malham-dale nestling just beneath us. Around us in the ling and moorland herbage, green cloudberry were numerous but no flowers were showing as yet. Only on the high mountain tops will the plants grow.

Behind the summit, in the hollow which runs down to a lone farmhouse, we had lunch. Here there was not a breath of wind and as the warm sun came out at intervals it was very pleasant. The sandwiches which had been put up by Alesia* tasted great, and savoured of the good rich substantial fare of Craven farmhouses.

We circled the head of the valley and over the craggy limestone tops we headed towards Attermire. Near the spot an old record says that sea pink grows in an upland field but I have yet to find it, or a person who has seen it. Sea plantain however does grow here beside the winding bridle path. Rabbits scuttled about everywhere as we climbed the hills and dropped into the limestone hollows. At each rise the wind met us with gusto. The sun had gone now so snaps were out of the question otherwise more pictures might have adorned these pages. Miles away however the day was bright and sunny. Over Skipton and the Craven lowlands the sun shone for hours while we were in shade.

By the holly fern rocks we stayed awhile to peep at the ferns and saw seven healthy roots, and so by devious ways we reached Attermire. Here meadow saxifrage leaves studded the ground in bud. Neither mossy saxifrage nor vernal sandwort was out yet. The latter grew in massive green rounded cushions and soon would be a show of pure white blossom. Early purple orchids dotted the turf between grey rocks with bright colour, and alpine penny cress was in full flower over the steep slopes. A kestrel flew out of the turreted crag, probably from its nest high up in a deep crevice.

Dew ponds are to be found all over these hills and by one we flushed out a pair of teals, but found no trace of a nest in the rough grass. By the puddly margin of the pond was a curlew's egg without shell, dropped there no doubt by some forlorn bird in passing.

Whitlow grass and thale cress were in flower as we dropped down to the top of Castleber, and after climbing the high wall and viewing Settle from the seat while we smoked a pipe of peace, with the owners below minus 2d each person, we climbed back and circled round and down into Settle. Then the quick beat of an internal combustion engine took us across the valley to Long Gill. Looking back later in the evening we saw Hinklehaugh sleeping in the twilight against a starlit sky ere it faded silently away into the shadows of the night.

Barnoldswick,
June 24th 1934.

*Alesia is Alice Frankland

Craven Herald, Friday, May 7, 1954

FINEST VIEW OF AIREDALE

CRAVEN NATURALISTS CLIMB RYELOAF

The Craven Naturalists and Scientific Association held their second outing of the summer on Saturday, when upwards of 20 members paid a visit to Ryeloaf, under the leadership of the president, Mr. W.B. Lord. After the long dry spell, the weather had broken greatly to the benefit of growing things, and although the morning skies had an ominous appearance and thunder was in the air, the afternoon brought spells of sunshine with a warm feeling of real spring.

Leaving the main road at the old toll-bar near Settle, the route was taken by Lodge Farm, and so by the green lanes into Scaleber road when the final ascent of Ryeloaf was made from just beyond Stockdale. In the woods near The Lodge the moist warm atmosphere gave the blackbirds and thrushes great power of song, to which the willow warblers now back from warmer climes added their sweet diminuendo. Violets and primroses, rather late this year, were beginning to peep in ever-increasing numbers from the banks. The vivid green of the larch trees was a joy to the eye, but many wind-seared Scots pines told of the havoc of the past winter, which to plant life of all kinds has been one of the most severe within living memory.

Cousin Mark Frankland on the ascent to Ryeloaf, May 13, 1934

A Black Villain

In a hawthorn tree by the wayside a carrion crow had built its nest, half the materials of which are composed of the bleached bones of sheep and rabbits, and once or twice a black villain was seen making its way across the brown fields. Wheatears bobbed about the walls, and above Stockdale farm, a green dish in the hills, many rooks were planing and gliding on the eddying wind currents.

Across, Ryeloaf stood up brown and bare in contrast to the white hills on this side of the valley, showing clearly the line of the Craven Fault. Cattle grazed the hillside, and the triangulation stone on the summit gleamed white in the sunshine.

The ascent from here was but a short climb and easily attained. The bogs were almost dry but the bog cotton grass – Eriophorum vaginatum – with its yellow flowers, was dotted about, waiting for the rains to come before it shows its white fluffy seed heads later in the year. Occasionally a meadow pipit flew up from the heather.

Unfortunately, the view from the summit, 1794 ft., was not too clear, but clear enough to show that from here one has probably the finest view of Airedale. High over the head of the valley one looks straight down to the industrial towns far beyond Skipton, where interest in Airedale, to the country lover, ceases. One has not seen the true beauty of Airedale till one has seen it from Ryeloaf on a clear day. Airton and Calton lay peacefully below Kirkby Fell, and beyond, Sharphaw and Crookrise looked very close. Apart from this, the view to the west and north is magnificent. Bowland Fells, Penyghent, Buckden Pike, Great Whernside and other peaks rear up their heads against the skyline.

In Abundance

The old name of this mountain as written in books of the 16th and 17th centuries, was Hinklehaugh, variously spelt Hinclehaugh, Hinklehaw and Hinklechew. This was a name which fitted in well with such noble names as Ingleborough, Penyghent and Whernside, until some "Peter Bell" came along and with his simple mind saw in it a resemblance to a ryeloaf, and so the good old, perhaps Gaelic, name is now forgotten. John Ray, the father of English botany, who visited this district centuries ago, recorded the cloudberry as growing, "on Hinklehaugh, near Settle."

It is still here, for the green leaves of this alpine bramble were just showing fresh growth among the rough tussocks near the summit cairn. Ray also recorded the sea pink here in 1690 as follows, "Prope Hinklehaugh and in Bleaberry Gill at the head of Stockdale fields near Settle." Since about 1870 it had been lost, but was found again by chance only a few years ago.

Below Stockdale the party left the road and returned by the path under Attermire, surely one of the finest limestone formations in Craven. Here the moist weather had brought out the snails (Helix nemoralis) which crept over the rocks in great abundance, carrying their many-banded shells in patterns of buff and brown. Barren strawberries were in flower among the short sweet grass. In the distance, a haze in the valley and sun on the tops appeared to lift up the far-away moorland knolls of Scoutber and Whelpstone Crag to twice their usual height as the party dropped down into Langcliffe and so by the high road back to Settle.

J.N.F.

A NORTH COUNTRY SHEEP SALE

by one who was there – September 26th 1932 – (Braida Garth)

Mutton, to most people, conjures up a savoury plate with a combination of mint sauce, but to the north country farmer it is thought of in a different form. He sees the swelling moorlands shrouded in mist, or swept by a fierce blizzard; of shearing time, dipping time, washing time, spaining* time, lambing time, and a host of other times connected with sheep in the cycle of the year. Most of all the sheep fair in September when he hopes that trade is good, and surplus stocks will bring him good return.

Many a north country farmer, whose spreading acres reach from mountain to mountain holds such a sale each year, and very few but the farmers know that it exists; but to visit one of these is well worth the time and trouble of climbing up to the remote fastness of the farmhouse croft where it is held.

September in the lowlands is thought of as a pleasant month but up here, if the sun does not come out in a cold bright gleam, the air has the tang of winter. Even when it does appear it is often swept away almost immediately by a blinding shower which hurls itself from the crags above.

*spaining = taking lambs from sheep

Typical dales farm sale

44

Such a day as this brought a hardy group of farmers together, each anxious to see what price gimmers, wethers and old ewes – called draft yows – would fetch. Motor cars, motor cycles, traps, cyclists and pedestrians came streaming along the only track to the homestead, far removed from any other form of civilization. Only one other house was visible in the great brown valley, and that two miles away at least. Here the road could go no further for, behind, great limestone crags hemmed it in. A great larch and pine wood ran up the slope to the foot of the scar as protection from the wind. Hazel copses and stunted ash and rowan trees grow on the crags, and above, up went the rocks, and moorland, and heather, till it terminates at an elevation of 2,414ft above sea level, the summit of Whernside. Here the mountain crags stood high above the lonely valley and frowned across at other crags, on other mountains miles away - except when the clouds came down and shrouded them in mist.

On a small hill top in the green croft were four or five rows of sheep pens, each pen containing from six to fifteen head. 'Why not have the pens in a more sheltered hollow?' says someone who may not, yes, must not be a farmer. Ah but there is wisdom in this; the sheep look bigger and are seen to better advantage on rising ground.

The sale is due to commence at 1.00p.m. but time is of little account up here, and at least an hour goes by before a movement is made to the pens. Farmers pass the time wandering round the numerous buildings, chatting with old friends and neighbours who live up to fifteen miles away. All are asked to go to dinner which is ready with a welcome for all comers. Whilst standing in a big shed the master of the farm came round. Spotting an acquaintance from over the hill he said to him, "Hed thi' dinner, Jack?". "Aye", says Jack, "I've hed a bit at horam". "Come an hev t'other bit," says the boss, "and then tha'll a hed thi dinner". This tickled the humour of the chatting groups who showed their appreciation in a general subdued chuckle.

By two o'clock the local auctioneer wanders quietly towards the pens, and the farmers group themselves on rails and temporary seats round the ring where the sheep are to be driven in, in batches. The auctioneer stands on an upturned wooden sheep trough and his clerk opens out a portable table beside him and rigs up a gigantic umbrella – at least five feet across – to keep the rain off his books. The shepherd puts on his oilskins, talking the while to his valuable dog which watches him intently. Though there is a brusqueness in his manner, there is a sturdy love behind it all. "Its nat t'fell today owd lass," he says. The beautiful brown eyes of the dog seem to understand as its tail

Typical Dales sheep sale

goes sideways with ever so slight a motion.

The first batch of gimmers is driven in, and many scores of weather beaten faces scan them intently. The cutting wind that sears their faces is forgotten as the auctioneer calls out. "What shall I ask for these? Thirty bob, twenty five, who'll give me a start with twenty? Nineteen bid, nineteen, nineteen shillings, nineteen and six, nineteen and a half, one pound, one pun, one pun, one and a half. Look at them gentlemen, beautiful skins, twenty two, twenty two and three, twenty two and six, twenty two and nine, twenty three, twenty and three, twenty three and six, twenty four, twenty four shillings, twenty four, twenty four, all down, and all down for all time at twen-tee-four, down at twenty four, twenty four shillings. Fred – Fred Benson." And so the sale goes on, regardless of the cold rain and wind that hisses past at intervals, then passes away, leaving the great hump-backed mountains across the valley as clear and defined as an oil-painting set against a background of grey packing clouds; but still the wind cuts like a knife.

Dry humour is rampant between the farmers, and the auctioneer creates fun as he calls individuals by name, joking about them now and again and thus keeping the group in good spirits, as batch after batch of sheep is drawn in, and disposed of. Lastly come the old ewes which have weathered many years on the mountains. They go to farms lower down, have one crop of lambs, and are then turned into mutton. Thus their lives are all prematurely ended.

The sale is at last completed. Is it home time? Oh no, for tea is ready and there are lots of things to talk about before each farmer goes back to his own homestead. In an out-house two long trestle tables are laden with a spread, which if not dainty is at least spotlessly clean and enough to spare for all who care to sit down. And most of the farmers do. Never lacking in these parts is this hospitality. Big plates of cheese and bread, huge currant loaves, pasties, big apple pies and sponge loaf covered every available space on the tables, and the women folk of the house are busy with the tea. Each farmer emerges in satisfied and amiable spirits, and eventually wanders off down the valley, in his car or on his cycle with a feeling that he has had a great day, and fondly hoping to be there again next year if he still lives.

Horton-in-Craven,
May 1933.

STONE WALLS OF CRAVEN

The notion of laying out dry stone walls across the Dales landscape occurred to man way back in the mists of pre-history, and traces of these first walls can still be discerned as low, often grass covered, linear banks. The rationale behind these first walls may have been simply what to do with all the loose stones that had been gathered up as new areas were being cleared for cultivation: a line of stones along the edge of a new field made more sense than great mounds piled up at intervals across the field. It would not have taken much for early folk to have realised that these linear works could also act as stock control and boundary features. Many of the curving, irregular walls of the valley bottoms date from the late monastic period when land was being managed in a systematic way, but the arrow straight walls marching up the fells were laid down in the great Enclosure Movement of the late 18th and early 19th centuries.
David S Johnson

Someone once said 'England without her hedgerows would not be England'. I say 'Craven without her stone walls would not be Craven'. Nothing against the hedgerows for I love them nonetheless and both in their own way are full of a certain romance and hold a history reaching back into days long gone by.

Wherever you go on the hills of Craven the stone walls, so to speak, will follow you. They run for miles across the highest and wildest moor; they climb the steepest mountain right to the summits standing almost end-ways up; swing across the steep breasts; dive into the gullies and out again, and so across the rocky fields to the next sheer dip. Look at them as they pattern out the hillsides into squares, rectangles, triangles and all sorts of mazy designs, and then think a little if you can about the human beings who built them, and why. The latter question is easy to answer; the former will never be answered. All we can say is the 'old folk'.

No doubt they were not all built at once but added to year by year as more and more common land was enclosed. And the men who built them were artists-craftsmen. Those dry wallers of the olden time are not of this age. Few new walls are built nowadays, but the old ones have to be repaired now and then and occasionally we do come across some old bearded veteran who can really put up a piece of dry wall that is a pleasure to look at and admire. But the men who built them in the first place, how proud they must have been of their job, for it had to be done methodically so that it was strong and enduring, otherwise, how could all those hundreds of miles of dry walls have withstood the wild storms that sweep over the Craven uplands, so long.

If we take notice we see that the biggest stones are put close to the bottom, and higher up 'throughs' are put in in rows to hold each side of the wall together. At the top, to bind the whole together is a line of top stones – locally called 'cap-stones', leaning one against the other. The master waller never picked up a stone twice, and as a rule never placed it in position above one if he could avoid it, and above all never robbed Peter to pay Paul by laying a stone in another spot after he had fixed it in position. One of the main things was to keep the middle well up with small broken stones called fillings. Every stone, no matter how rough has its face, and this the builder could see at a glance. If at all possible the stones were laid end in and end out.

Look at a dry stone wall and think of the labour involved. Each stone has had to be handled and examined separately, for even though nothing was done twice over there was no rush or haste attached to it. Like everything the old folks did it was done slowly, sturdily and deliberately.

And why is Craven so full of stone walls? There are many reasons. First and foremost is that stone is everywhere abundant and handy, and you can tell by a glance at walls in any area whether the geological structure of the ground is limestone, gritstone, slate or any other rock, for Craven has a great variety of different rocks. Another reason is that on these wild, wind-swept hills and moors, hedges would in many spots never grow, or if they did they would no doubt be almost useless for fences capable of turning stock.

No doubt you will ask how long these walls will last. As far as we are concerned they will last forever if kept in decent repair. Gaps fall in them at times through various causes and must needs be rebuilt, so there will always be a bit of dry walling left for the farmers and shepherds. One of the fastest weathering stones is limestone, and when we are told that limestone weathers an inch in ten thousand years, it will be a different world ere even the limestone walls are weathered down to mere lines of carbonate of lime.

Cripple Hole. Photo: Jill Sykes

Sometimes the lowland people look at these walls and wonder. They think they are very bleak and uninteresting and no doubt to anyone not acquainted with the real wide-open spaces they are. But to a native of the hills they mean everything. It is the walls that keep his stock at home and divide his farm from the endless fells. There is nothing bleak about them to him. He would not exchange his walls for all the hedgerows in England. They were among the very first things he ever saw, and to him no other form of field border can ever equal them.

Sheep in any district are often wont to stray, and on the hills of Craven they cannot creep through hedges as they do in many districts. They have another way however. They are often excellent jumpers and many can jump a wall with the ease of a goat. If these sheep are taken to a district of hedges they are baffled and never think of creeping and in like manner lowland sheep have no idea about jumping a wall. Sheep are often the cause of much trouble to the farmers by causing huge gaps to fall when jumping the walls. To prevent this many of the fields are run together by means of 'cripple holes'. These are holes in the walls through which a sheep can comfortably walk and so allowing the sheep to wander in several fields but not the cattle. Visitors to the hills sometimes use these holes by creeping through them and so save climbing. Probably nine out of ten do not know their real use.

Another kind of hole often built into walls is the 'smoot' hole. These are placed at intervals along the foot of the wall and are small square holes for the use of rabbits and hares to enable them to get from one field to another without jumping. They are used very much as may be seen by the beaten tracks which lead to them. Rabbits on the hills often bring in a good income for the farmer during the winter months.

To enable people to cross the walls there are stiles. Not the kind of stiles one sees in hedges but flag steps built into the wall with a narrow gap at the top to enable the legs to go through. One can follow the footpath through the fields for miles crossing each wall by the stone stiles or 'stees' as the country people call them.

Perhaps the most romantic wall in Craven is the one known as the 'Celtic Wall', which is situated on the hills mid-way between Stackhouse and Feizor. To what period it belongs or the reason for it being there has long been lost down the ages; but there it stands for all who wish to see and guess, perhaps rather hazily, why it was built so strongly. What is now left of it is built of limestone and is five feet through at the base tapering to three and a half feet at the top and stands perhaps six-foot high. The remains of it still reach for 25 yards in good condition, and traces of it in the form of tumbledown bits can be seen in several places some distance away so it must have been much longer at one time. We will leave the Celtic wall to withstand the centuries to come as it has withstood the centuries past. Each summer the wild thyme and rockrose blooms about it, and each winter the storms beat against it; yet still it stands. If only the meddlesome litter lout, and destructive sightseers will leave it alone, many many generations of the future will continue to pay homage to it, as its known history sinks forever further and further back into the years gone by.

Another kind of wall we often see in Craven is one built at right angles in the middle of a field. These walls are made for shelter for stock for in many places there is nothing to intercept the wild cold blasts. These walls are called 'Bield Walls', a northern word which means shelter walls. A bieldy spot is a sheltered spot in Craven.

Walls after all are not such uninteresting things as people from the hedgerow counties often think. There is a romance about them that we only half know, as we look across at them hanging precariously over deep ravines or thrusting themselves solidly over the mountain tops. The walls of Craven were built with a purpose, to withstand the centuries, and after all, if they are not what one might call beautiful, they are certainly good to look at.

Barnoldswick, early 1930s.

A WEEK IN SOUTH WEST ENGLAND

As a respected botanist Frankland was invited by Sir Maurice and Lady Abbot-Anderson to Lyme Regis to visit botanical sites. He was taken by them to visit Miss Miller, artist and botanist, who lived at Burnham, from where they made further botanical excursions. Frankland's stoical nature vividly emerges as he makes the journey from Barnoldswick to Lyme Regis on a motor bike of the time, and is undaunted either by early rising, bad weather or by machine breakdown.

Maureen Ellis

June 6th 1931

On this date, June 6th 1931, South West England was to me an unknown country. Imagination had woven many flitting pictures before the mind, but whether they were anywhere near what I was about to see had yet to be seen. I was to be the guest of Sir Maurice Abbot-Anderson and his good lady at their cottage which looks out over Lyme Regis Bay. My hopes ran high as I ruminated on my prospect and of the many new flowers which I would be taken to see.

At 3.00a.m. I looked out of the window. It was raining in torrents, and so I got back into bed. The downpour was still in being at 4.30a.m. but I went downstairs and had breakfast after washing and shaving, and then read 'The Innocents Abroad' until the weather cleared. Just before 10.00a.m. there was a slight break in the wind and rain, so I decided to start, and was away soon after. It was still spotting a bit and the roads were swimming, but 'wind or rain, snow or blow' said I, 'I'll reach the sunny south' before the end of the day.

On leaving Keighley I ran into mist which continued more or less thickly all the way to Buxton. Although the day had never been really fair, near Buxton the rain came on very heavily, but I did not shelter as I had little time to spare for the long journey. The hills above Glossop were a fine sight, and it was rather clearer there, so I got a good view of the deep moorland glens which I considered to be more like the Lake District than any hills I have seen in

Yorkshire. Buxton itself is very nice but I was not at all impressed with the surrounding country. Just a medley of big undulating tree-less fields with lime kilns and dumps here and there. Beyond Buxton I had a fine spell of sunshine but my hopes were soon shattered by another violent shower. During the shower I noticed Wood spurge growing rampantly by the roadsides and in the woods, so I got off my motor-cycle to examine the plant, as I had not seen it previously.

Again the sun shone out, and just as I was thinking how glorious it was my luck was dead against me, for although the weather still kept glorious and sunny, I ran on to flooded roads. They were shallow at first and I splashed merrily through, and then the water began to get deeper with a strong current against me almost like – in fact, quite like – a river, and not a small one at that – it was fully a yard deep. Then the motor-cycle 'conked' out. Who could blame it or any machine in such circumstances? I was in the middle of the flood stream and the only way was to go on. I moved to the side and scrambled on to a bank to which the road joined luckily without a ditch. By this means I could push the bike – up to the saddle in water – and walk, or rather stagger along the bank. It was hard work, and hot, as the sun poured down on the rushing floods, and I wore two macs besides my haversack and vasculum. The rushing torrent at times almost carried the bike away, and at times I thought I should never get out. However, by thoroughly soaking myself I eventually won through. In many places the water was rushing in torrents through the gate-ways as it swept the river over the fields and into the road. I must have come at least a mile in this way. After reaching dry ground I cleaned the water out of the magneto which had been the cause of my stoppage no doubt. Exhaust pipes full of water also helped to put on the brake. After some difficulty and not a little delay I got a start with the help of two men who gave a willing hand in pushing me. I had wasted the major portion of two hours here. When the engine started, water spouted out of the exhaust pipes like a hose-pipe in full blow, and it took some time to clear all the working parts of water, and to get the engine running smoothly once again. I passed though Lichfield about 4.30p.m. and admired the cathedral. Then on via Warwick, Stratford-on-Avon, Cheltenham and Stroud to Bath.

The country around Painswick and Stroud in Gloucestershire is very beautiful. At Bath there were flying showers again but I pushed on, hoping to make Lyme Regis before it was too late to knock up the good knight and his lady, should they have retired thinking that I would not arrive that day.

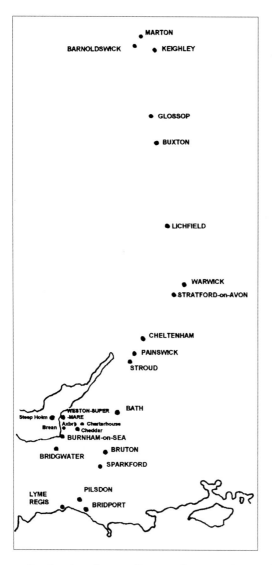

Frankland's motor bike journey and some of the sites he visited with Sir Maurice and Lady Abbot-Anderson.

By the time I got to Bruton, however, it was dark. I then decided to put up for the night. No accommodation was to be had in Bruton so I went on to the little village of Sparkford, where I was fortunate enough to obtain a very good place for the night with Mr Pittard, the village blacksmith. After a good supper of ham at 11.00p.m. I then chatted with Mr Pittard, who was a very intelligent young man, until 12 o'clock when we went to bed.

June 7th

I arose at 7.30a.m. and had a good breakfast before taking to the road at 8.40a.m. or so, heading for Lyme Regis. The room in which I had slept at Sparkford was very quaint and old-fashioned, with a sloping under-drawn ceiling, and a rickety stone stairway winding up from the kitchen. I am not sure whether the house was thatched or not but I think so. Mrs Pittard was a very nice woman and said that if ever I passed that way again I had to be sure and look in to see them. Their little boy gave me a bit of the Zomerzet dialect, such as counting, – Von – doo – tree – vour – vive – zix – zeven etc.

The rain poured down all the way to Lyme Regis, but I had not very far to go, so I did not mind very much. Over the hills just before I got there I could see very little for mist, but what I could see of the countryside was very luxuriant and beautiful.

I arrived at Lyme Regis at about 10.30a.m. and leaving my motor-cycle at the Royal Lion Hotel Garage, where Sir Maurice keeps his car, I went down to Madeira Cottage where I had a hearty welcome. My first view of the sea was most impressive; it was down the narrow street of Lyme, and the rich green and blue shades, even on this dull day, I have never seen to better effect since I was at Douglas I.o.M. in 1924.

The rain still held sway outside and the mist thickened over the sea, so we stayed indoors until after lunch when we decided to go out rain or shine. By then…

June 12th

After rising I packed up a parcel of plants each for Fred and John, and by 8.40a.m. we were off for what proved to be a crowning day in Zomerzet. The weather, though rather dull early, soon brightened and we basked in warm sunshine afterwards. Via Up Lyme, past St. Mary's Woods we went, and soon we were speeding along the wide main road for Bridgwater and Burnham-on-Sea. Before we had gone far we could see the rounded line of the Mendips in the far distance; the hills we were to traverse ere the day was out. Pretty villages, verdant fields and meadows, green woods, and country houses amid their ancestral parks were left behind as we sped on via Axminster, Chard and Taunton.

Passing through Bridgwater, a very fine town, we arrived at Burnham. We went along the front in the car and had a fine view of the Severn Estuary. S. Wales was visible, and immediately between rose the steep rocky island of

Steep Holme, famous for its paeony. Behind was the much lower island called Flat Holme. Turning into Stoddam Road we sought out Miss Miller who was to take us to see the rarities of Somerset. Sir Maurice of course knows them all, but deems it right to see the Millers when taking a stranger to see plants of Somerset which the Millers are unpaid and voluntary guardians of. Botanists like these belong to what might be called the 'Inner Circle' of plant lovers and if one of these gives a stranger's name as genuine, then the whole countryside is at his command. I was glad also to be considered one of this 'Inner Circle'.

At the house called 'Audrey', No. 19, we stopped and soon found Miss Miller, who was in the garden. Her brother was away on a botanical tour in Teesdale. I was introduced to her, a very nice lady indeed with no 'side' whatever. Her knowledge of plants I soon gathered was very far-reaching. Miss Miller never pushed herself forward with opinions she could not substantiate.

Sir Maurice and Lady Abbot-Anderson, June 1931

First of all we looked round her garden and rockery, in which she specialises in wild plants. It was quite an education to me for I saw several plants I had not seen before, and but for this garden I may never have viewed them for many years, perhaps not at all. Amongst them were Sisyrinchium angustifolium, S. californicum, Romulea parviflora, Ajuga genevensis, Myosurus minimus, Caper spurge, Field gromwell, Cypripedium calceolus (not in flower), Dianthus caesius, Polycarpon tetraphyllum, Paeonia corallina, Dryas octopetala and the rare Meadow sage, S. pratensis beside many more just as interesting.

Romulea was in seed, but it grows nearby in a wild state. The flowers are of very short duration and in many years do not open unless the day on which they are ready to bloom is sunny. The seeds are very peculiar and curl down until they bury themselves in the ground. Ajuga genevensis was obtained in Cornwall along with Polycarpon, and she gave me roots of both. The Ajuga is a beautiful plant with brilliant deep blue flowers. The Paeonia was originally gathered on Steep Holme but Miss Miller says it is now very rare there, and only occurs on one inaccessible cliff. I noticed the Field gromwell and saw that it was the same plant I had found near the Chesil Bank on Tuesday last.

In a vase on the table in the hall were specimens of the Dwarf orchis, Green man orchis, Spider orchis and Cephalanthera ensifolia received from Hampshire some little time before. We then started on our botanical round of the Somersetshire wild plants. We had not far to go however before we got out of the car to view our first plant. It was Trigonella, growing on short turf near the tennis courts by the margin of the sand-hills. There was only a tiny bit so I did not ask for a specimen.

Then we walked down a path by which there was a notice board, 'To the Shore', but before we had gone above a hundred yards we turned through a gate marked 'Private' which led to the sand-hills, now used as a golf-course. Immediately through the gate was a steep sandy bank massed with Oenothera odorata, quite a different plant to O. biennis and new to me. I have never seen O. odorata on the Southport sand-hills. The flowers that had passed their best had turned to a beautiful bronze red. Festuca uniglumis too was common on the bank. The rounded sand-hills just past this bank were clothed with bushes and trees of natural growth and it was here we were to see one of our finest sights.

On a grassy copse-covered knoll we peeped among the bushes and soon found the bold spikes of the much-coveted Lizard orchis in bud. The tall thick stems and long rounded leaves shone bright and glossy, and you may imagine what a great thrill it was to me. Among the bushes on this grassy knoll we located at least twenty plants. After filling myself with this fine spectacle we left and went back to the car. Miss Miller says the Lizard orchis has been known on this knoll for at least forty years, yet it grew in quite a different place to where I should have expected to find it. This shows how different a plant appears to the mind when reading of it against it being actually viewed in situ. I expected to have been led through some green luxuriant forest of tall beech and oak trees to find the Lizard orchis rearing up its waving head among beds of dying hyacinth leaves, and bare chalky patches here and there. Miss Miller says children often find it when hunting for lost balls, and pluck it, but so long as the roots remain unmolested the plants will continue to bloom. I shall never forget the sight of the first Lizard orchis I ever saw growing in England, at Burnham-on-Sea in Somerset. Butterflies were plentiful, and I saw many that were new to me. Sir Maurice pointed out the female of the small blue.

Returning to the car we took the road towards Weston-super-Mare, and crossed a level district of marshy meadows with ditches between. Many of the meadows were flooded, and several portions of the road were inundated but not very deeply, so we easily got through them. Shelducks were sunning themselves by the ditch-sides, and made a very pretty picture, while waterhens flew about in all directions in front of the car. Before we actually left Burnham however Miss Miller showed us a Lepidium latifolium growing on a bank by the road. It was not yet in flower, but looked quite unlike any Lepidium I have seen before. It had thick green leaves which were very broad. My specimen labelled L. latifolium from Suffolk is certainly not correct.

On our left we could see Steep Holme not far away in the estuary, and in front in the distance was Brean Down (home of the white rock rose) standing out clearly defined against a blue summer sky.

We arrived at Weston-super-Mare and leaving the car we wandered along to try and find Equisetum variegatum. We turned along a path by a big bus park and in a wet hollow Scirpus rufus grew very finely. Near the station there was a long marshy pond surrounded by hen and duck pens, and twisting our way through wire netting we got to the water. After a long search interrupted by the screech of train whistles and the quack of ducks, we gave it up, as we could not be sure of any horse-tail we saw as being E. variegatum. It was rather early for this plant though, so perhaps we may have seen young plants. E. hyemale was there in plenty and not to be mistaken – also E. palustre and pratense. By the pens was a fine plant of Sisymbrium orientale and numerous Musk thistles.

We left Weston and went back along the road towards Burnham. By a disused quarry under Purn Down – now red with Spur Valerian – we had lunch and then moved off for a foray on Purn. Climbing up the steep rocky and bushy sides of the quarry we soon saw new things, for here Orobanche minor was well represented, also the rather rare Arenaria tenuifolia growing along with the thyme-leafed species. At the top, on the open downland and amongst the bushes which flanked the edges were rock-roses in profusion - a glorious sight. The white H. polifolium, the common, and hybrids between the two were frequent. The white rock-rose was very beautiful to me, but perhaps more so because it was new. The flowers were white with a yellow spot at the base of each petal.

Before we reached the open downland the heat was intense as the sun poured down on the slope. Butterflies of many species fluttered about and I saw several burnet moths with two spots, one of which became quite tame, for it crawled about on my hands and jacket. Brean Down stood out quite clear a few miles away. The white and yellow rock roses also occur on Brean Down, but a curious fact about it is that no hybrids are to be found there.

Broadcast over the open downland grew Trinia vulgaris among the rock roses, and we saw many Bee orchids on the grassy limestone ledges. On our return by a farther but easier route, we saw the Musk storksbill growing under a limestone ledge, but there were only a few very tiny plants. Dropwort was there too. Away in the opposite direction to Brean Down was a pointed peak called Brent Knoll. By a pond near the road we saw Celery-leaved crowfoot. After our fill of Purn Down we once more drove off in the car, this time to Axbridge and the Mendips.

Arriving at Axbridge and passing through its narrow streets we were not long before we stopped again by the end of a narrow rough lane. Sir Maurice said, "This is 'Depauperata' Lane", and so we went to see a rare sedge. Carex depauperata was located amongst the rank grass by the side of the lane. There was quite a lot of it, and Purple gromwell also grew there.

Leaving 'Depauperata Lane' we turned to the left where the rolling Mendips stretched away above us, for we were now close to the slopes. We turned up another road from the main and soon began to climb up amid the extensive copse woods that clothed their slopes and crest. Miss Miller pointed out the

Sir Maurice Abbot-Anderson and Norman Frankland

spot where a Wryneck has nested for several successive years. The tiny valley on our left looked very cosy. A small hollow nestled under the woods and it was mostly composed of ploughed fields like little gardens, each holding many rows of different crops, and were spread out before us in a mazy pattern. There were sheltered little cottages in this tiny valley too.

At last we reached the top of the wooded slopes – reminiscent of many limestone woods in Yorkshire – and were on the rolling summit of the Mendips. Here too were copses and fragrant meadows, and altogether the uplands were very fertile. The road then ran open to the fields, only narrow but with a good tarred surface. We had many gates to open as we passed.

We left the car by the roadside and walked down a field to the top of a gill where the stream began, as it emerged from a meadow-hollow and then trickled down between bushy banks. Passing through a gate we wandered through the long grass of the meadow, taking care to keep close to the wall. Here was the Meadow saffron (leaves and seeds) among the thick grass. Across the small hollow and some little distance away, Tinings Farm to which the meadow belonged.

On the slope near the edge of a copse we came across the object of our visit, Vicia orobus, tangling itself amongst the rich grass. There were several clumps and they looked beautiful in their natural habitat. The flowers were of a delicate flesh colour and on a closer examination were streaked with purple. It is certainly one of the prettiest vetches I have ever seen, the colour being quite unique. The Wood vetch is very near it in growth but not in colour. The Wood vetch though, has long branched tendrils and grows much bigger, while Vicia orobus has nothing but a short point where the tendril should be. On searching the slope further, Sir Maurice found two plants with pure white flowers and he was delighted as neither he nor Miss Miller had seen it with white petals before. This is the only station in Somerset, and it is not found in any of the bordering counties; it is also very rare in England. I was therefore delighted to see it here.   We returned to the car and admired the fine view as we partook of Devonshire cider in the warm sunshine. Around were the green tops of the Mendips rising very little higher than where we stood, and down the gap in the hills where the stream flowed we saw a beautiful sunlit picture – framed by the hills and the sky. We saw the wide plain below, with Brean Down, the Severn Estuary, and beyond and across – South Wales. A pair of French Partridges were out on the grass.

We had not gone far along the road in the car when we saw a group of men in a meadow, cutting and carting away two barrows which had long broken the smoothness of the turf. There were cars and other men apart from the workmen, who we thought were investigating the work, and were on the lookout for relics of a by-gone age.

Arriving at Charterhouse, a pretty hamlet in the hills, we stayed awhile by a little bridge across a small mossy dam. It was a quaint little structure and one of the prettiest I have seen so we took snaps of it. Mine did not come out well as my camera was a new one and turned out more or less of a dud. On the farm wall nearby was an abundance of Rusty-back fern. By a rough field we again stopped the car and saw Carex montana, and Sir Maurice found a clump of Ajuga, which we believe to be A. reptans, var. pseudo alpina. As the road again ran through fields we had two gates to open, and then we arrived on to the main Bath and Bristol Road.

We turned to the right and were soon speeding down the ever-narrowing hollow that leads to the Cheddar Gorge, famous for its cheese, but to me far more famous for its pink. At last we got down to where the rocky screes went straight up from the road on each side and here Sir Maurice and I got out of the car to walk down through the gorge to the village of Cheddar. Lady Abbot-Anderson and Miss Miller went forward in the car to wait for us down below. Under the bushes we saw Epipactis coming up which may have been, and looked rather like, E. atro-purpurea.

Limestone polypody was also here, and Early purple orchis still in flower. Sir Maurice led me through a gateway to see the Mossy saxifrage in its most southerly station in England, and nearby we saw Herb Robert with white flowers. I saw my first Sulphur butterfly and later on I saw many more down the gorge flitting about in the sunshine. When we returned to the road we met a family party, a man, a woman and a boy, coming slogging and sweating up the road. The man carried his hat in his hand, and wiping the perspiration off his brow said to us, "Can you tell me how far we are from the Rock of Ages?" We did not know as we had never heard of it in this vicinity. We could not help him, but we afterwards learned that he had passed it far away down the gorge and how much further he went we could only guess.

Here the sides of the rocky gorge were clothed with extensive woods of larch and pine, fringed about with hazel thickets ere they narrowed into the actual cliff-walled gorge. We rounded the bend, and here we came across another group of people and a car by the roadside. They were preparing tea and a cyclist stood near by. As we passed one of them said "Could you tell us where the Rock of Ages is?" Again we did not know, but promised them that we should be sure to find out as soon as we could, as it must be a very interesting place – popular anyway. I said in a dreamy way that I had long considered all the rocks to be rocks of ages, whilst Sir Maurice more bluntly remarked that he was very sorry not being able to help them with the Rock of Ages but he knew that this particular rock wasn't cleft for him; and so we went on with our botanising. Later we discovered that the Rock of Ages was so-named by the fact that a certain lady (I forget her name) was long ago caught up here in a storm. She sheltered in one of the many clefts in the rocks and there, with the wind and rain howling about her, she composed the old famous hymn, "Rock of ages cleft for me". This is fact, and periodically services are held there.

We saw a lot of rocks and clefts before we reached Cheddar, but which was the "Rock of Ages" we still have to find out.

Welsh stonecrop was everywhere in bud, and Rusty back fern was common on the rocks. Red valerian was also abundant further down near Cheddar, whilst Welsh poppies grew up the steep screes. By now we were in the actual gorge and here the screes almost disappeared and giant cliffs took their place, rising sheer from the tar macadam of the roadway to many hundreds of feet above. One appeared at times to be in a deep gulf with nothing but a winding patch of sky overhead. It was most impressive as we went twisting and turning down the road, each corner bringing some new and wonderful view. I have never seen a gorge like it, but then, every gorge is different and has a charm of its own. To say that it was more wonderful, and grander than our Yorkshire gorges (or less so) would not be fair, for where Cheddar is lacking in many points our gorges bring them out to the full, and vice-versa. Ling Gill in upper Ribblesdale, although it has the same frowning limestone cliffs, lacks the bare grandeur of Cheddar, whilst Cheddar has no wild mountain stream and foaming waterfalls like those which line the deep gulf of Ling Gill. Ling Gill holds the laurels for quiet seclusion and wild natural beauty, as it is miles from the nearest road in the heart of the mountains. For every one person who visits Ling Gill, thousands must pass through Cheddar. Malham Cove holds a dreamy peacefulness, whilst Gordale Scar has a wilder ruggedness than Cheddar.

After scanning the cliffs we detected our first tuft of Dianthus caesius. It was easy of access, so I clambered up and found it to hold five of the daintiest flowers one could ever wish to see. You may imagine my delight when I first beheld such a rare and beautiful plant on its native rocks. As the sun shone on it I took two photos of it which did not turn out too well. Further down, all the way to Cheddar, the cliffs were splashed with its pink flowers; most, I was glad to see on inaccessible cliffs, but also commonly just above our heads where one could easily reach it. Where there was an open space of screes and small terraced cliffs I scrambled up again, and viewed many fine bunches within easy reach. Time and again I smelled their sweet fragrance as I plucked several specimens. Here I found plenty growing high up on the loose stones of the screes, but well out of the way of all but the athletic climber. Here also was the Nettle-leaved bell-flower, but of course not yet out.

It was now 6.30p.m. and the sun shone athwart crags ever-beetling, and frowning above us. The light and shade on the massive rifted rocks was a never-to-be-forgotten picture.

We now entered the lovely village of Cheddar, and were among houses while we were still between the beetling crags. Near a house door was a fine plant of Cardamine impatiens which Miss Miller says comes up where-ever ground is stirred during cave excavations.

There were many posters inviting one to visit the caves, 'electric light throughout', and some of them went straight in from the tarred road with lights dangling from the rocky roofs. One poster read 'Prehistoric Man on View', which made us laugh. We afterwards found out it was a skeleton, a thing which a schoolboy once described as being a man with the inside out, and the outside off. We did not go to see it.

There was an artificially made pond in the centre of the village. It was quite a big one ringed round with all kinds of English and foreign water plants. It looked very pretty in its setting of cliff and wood, with cottages nestling beneath. We had tea in Cheddar, in a beautiful tea-garden under the blue sky. Fountains were playing near us, pretty mossy fountains that looked so old and natural, and waterfalls rushed over the rocks at the upper end, then went bubbling along among green ferns by the side of grassy lawns. Winding paths, cliffs and yew trees surrounded us, and flowers peeped out from every quarter. The air was sweet and fragrant, and altogether it was most pleasant, but we guessed that it would be a deuced place for midges, when the shadows lengthened on the smart lawns. In a tea-room nearby every table held a vase of Orchis praetermissa, so we deduced that it was a common plant about here.

Axbridge was only a mile or two distant, and so we motored on to Burnham to take Miss Miller home. I was glad indeed to have met her and hoped it would not be the last time. She said with genuine feeling that it was a delight to take me round her beloved Somerset.

We said goodbye, and were soon speeding back to Lyme Regis. On our left, after leaving Bridgwater we could see Glastonbury Tor quite plainly away in the distance.

Some five or six miles from Lyme we ran into mist which continued all the way back. This was due no doubt to the proximity of the sea and we thought it might have been misty all day here. We found however that it had been fine and sunny, and the mist had only appeared in the evening. One remarkable thing to me about the Mendips is that on the whole length of them there is scarcely a visible outcrop of rock; they appear to be round rolling downs, yet, in the middle of all this smooth green pasturage there is one vast gorge cutting its way into the hills. I think it must have been formed by some volcanic action which rent the hills in bygone ages.

June 13th

My last day in the south. On first looking out I found it to be bright and sunny, and surely, I thought, the weather must be improving now that I am about to return home.

Before breakfast Lady Anderson and I took a short walk on to the Cob, a tiny harbour at the west end of the town, hoary with antiquity. Today I could get a good view of the bay, terminating miles away in Portland Bill just visible in the hazy distance. I believe the Bay of Lyme Regis has been compared favourably with the Bay of Naples in the sunny Mediterranean Sea. The harbour is a very tiny quaint place, and was much more used formerly than now. One could see by the thick walls that many additions and alterations had been made since it was first built many hundreds of years ago. On a piece of waste ground near by, Monmouth landed during the time of his rebellion, and Lady Anderson pointed out the house where Jane Austen lived and stayed, and also houses and places figuring in Jane Austen's stories.

On a bank by the promenade, where no houses are yet built, owing to the slippery composition of the Blue Lias we saw plenty of Petasites fragrans, and one Bee orchis amongst the grass. This we carefully concealed.

After breakfast I went up to the garage for the motor-cycle, but could not start it owing to it having stood a week after having got thoroughly soaked. I had to take out the points of the magneto and free the rocker arm which was sticking. Eventually, at 11.00am. we were ready for the road, for Lady Anderson and Sir Maurice were coming so far with me and we were to have our last botanising foray among Orchis incarnata.

We went through Bridport, and soon afterwards turned off to the left on a rough by-road which brought us to the summit of the Downs. We were 800ft. above sea level, and what a wonderful view we had. I should think we could see the greater part of the county of Dorset. Lady Anderson pointed out Pilsdon Pen, 903ft. above sea level which is the highest point in Dorset. Pen is an Old English word meaning head, thus Penyghent = Head of the Open Dale; Pen-y-Pass = Head of the Pass; Pendle = Head of the Dale. I did not expect to meet this word in Dorset. We passed a huge earthwork which I would have liked to explore, had we had time. I think this hill is known as Egton or Eggardon Hill.

Deep coombes swept down below us to the vale and its cornfields and green pastureland. What a sensation this downland country brought to me with its knolls and earthworks. Through my mind ran passages from the writings of Richard Jefferies. I could visualise many of them now, yet these were not Jefferies' Downs. "The most commanding Down" wrote Jefferies, "is crowned by a grassy mound, the remnants of an ancient earthwork".

Over the rutty roads open to the hills and through gates we went till we began to descend to a stretch of marshy fields with places covered with willow trees, and copse wood, and thick hawthorn hedges fringing the swamps. We were now in the haunt of the Orchis incarnata and on leaving the car and motor-cycle we came on the plant in plenty among the thick marsh grass. Its rich flesh-coloured flowers were very striking and pretty. Orchis praetermissa was here too, but I saw no plants new to me as I know Orchis incarnata well in the North. There were great masses of needle greenweed growing amongst the gorse bushes. I saw a host of butterflies and one big dragonfly, and also a small brown bird which I think was a grasshopper warbler. I think, too , it got off a nest as it ran through the grass like a mouse before it flew away. We could not find it however.

It was beautiful here as we sat on the grass and had lunch beside the car. Lady Anderson took two photos of Sir Maurice and me as we sat on the grass. In front of us the rolling downs swept away towards the sea which lay beyond; about us the rich land of marsh and copsy hollow; and rearwards on the hill above thick woods and plantations and twisted rose-garlanded lanes, for the roses had begun to bloom. We said goodbye to Poorstock, for this was its name, and went through the winding lanes, and down a long road which leads from the uplands to Beaminster, where I said au revoir to my kind hosts and proceeded on my way towards the bleaker northlands. I was very sorry indeed to say goodbye to this fair land of Wessex, but all good things come to an end, and though I greeted it in rain I was glad to leave it in sunshine.

I intended to go home by a different route and stay the night at my cousin's at Chester, but good fortune did not favour me again. I got a long way on the road when my primary chain broke and I was delayed two hours. Fortunately there was a garage not far away but it was 8.30p.m. by the time I was on the road again. This was in Somerset, and as the evening shadows fell over the land I once more went through the Cheddar Gorge, this time up it on a motor-cycle. I stopped in its dusky depths and had a last peep at the Cheddar Pink which I could just discern hanging on its native ledges. Over the main road to Bath, and then with lamp alight I pushed on and on along strange roads, till near Lasborough in Gloucestershire, when one day was almost verging on the next, I was lucky to find a lodging for the night. 'Twas a roadside café and garage in rather a wild and lonely spot, but a very good place. Here I got a pot of tea, and had supper consisting of a cold chop, bread & butter and tomato, followed by pasty, the whole of which the good Lady Abbot-Anderson had so kindly packed into my vasculum. It was not long before I went to bed, and finding it very comfortable was soon fast asleep.

June 14th

By 9.00a.m. I was sitting down to breakfast in a spacious dining room. Bacon, eggs and marmalade was my fare and I thoroughly enjoyed it. Paying up was the next item and this cost me 6/6. The morning was bright although the roads were damp, telling of a shower over-night. Soon after it tried to rain a little as I zoomed along the road but I did not feel pessimistic.

My expectations were more than realised for I had a fine sunny day until I was well towards home. Near Stroud in Gloucestershire, where the road runs open to a common, I found a quantity of Sainfoin growing in patches amongst the grass. I had never viewed this plant in situ before, and it looked very pretty growing here on its native heath.

I came home the same way I went, except that I made a short detour to see Kenilworth Castle, a huge sombre pile of red masonry. There were crowds of people about it in the sunshine, which made me think it was a very popular resort in this part of the country. After passing through Lichfield I travelled the road where a week ago I was water-logged, but passed the spot today quite dry. I secured specimens of Wood spurge from a wayside wood, and then carried on over the moors of Derbyshire and the Peak District to Yorkshire, Keighley, Skipton and Horton.

At Keighley the skies were very dull and rain was in the air, but it did not start really in earnest till I was almost at Horton-in-Craven. Near Marton, three miles from my home, my back tyre punctured and went down, but with the aid of the pump it carried me home, so I considered myself fortunate. I arrived at Horton at 5.15p.m., had tea, and finished the evening at Barnoldswick. Soon after I arrived home it rained as it very rarely rains in England, or even in Craven, and I was thankful that I had been lucky enough to have a fine day for my long ride.

Before I went down south I thought I should be able to compare Yorkshire with Dorset, and say without doubt which was the prettier part of England, but now, although it is nice to compare, I cannot say which district has it. It would be unfair to say either, as they are both in Grade A. From a sentimental standpoint Craven comes first as my land of dreams, but Dorset, Devon and Somerset certainly hold many reasons why they should be considered three of the most romantic and prettiest counties in England. May they never be marred by the advance (or decline) of civilization – as some parts of Yorkshire are – so that in hundreds of years hence when I am no more and probably long forgotten, some other lover of the wild may go from the Craven Hills as

I have done, and see all the beautiful flowers growing just as they are now, and bring back with him to Craven an echo of my gleanings – sunny memories of the beautiful south-lands.

J.N.F. in pensive mood

and learnt much

In one
three of the main
meet, each of them
different kind of
as crystal, for it
the limestone hills;
very brown, telling
is on the moors
the third runs slow
water and high
full of water lilie..
mossy plank, and
the very appropriate